Little SHARK

Little SHARK

Anne Rockwell

Pictures by Megan Halsey

SCHOLASTIC INC.

New York Toronto London Auckland Sydney
Mexico City New Delhi Hong Kong Buenos Aires

ISBN 0-439-80376-4

Text copyright © 2005 by Anne Rockwell.
Illustrations copyright © 2005 by Megan Halsey.
All rights reserved. Published by Scholastic Inc.,
557 Broadway, New York, NY 10012,
by arrangement with Walker Publishing Company, Inc.
SCHOLASTIC and associated logos
are trademarks and/or registered trademarks
of Scholastic Inc.

12 11 10 9 8 7 6 5 4 3 2   5 6 7 8 9 10/0

Printed in the U.S.A.   40

First Scholastic printing, September 2005

The artwork for this book
was created with
watercolors and colored pencils
on watercolor paper and bristol.
The backgrounds were painted
with watercolors
on gessoed illustration board.

The artist would like to thank
Peter Noah for his assistance.

Book design by Nicole Gastonguay

For Christian & Tudy
—A.R.
For Steve & Tim &
Miss Renee & Marty
—M.H.

In the dark deepness of the sea
Little Shark is born,
along with his forty-nine brothers and sisters.
He's not very big—only about ten inches long.

The huge mother shark swims away

as soon as all her little sharks are born.

So do Little Shark's forty-nine brothers and sisters.

Little Shark is all alone,

on his own in the deep and dangerous sea.

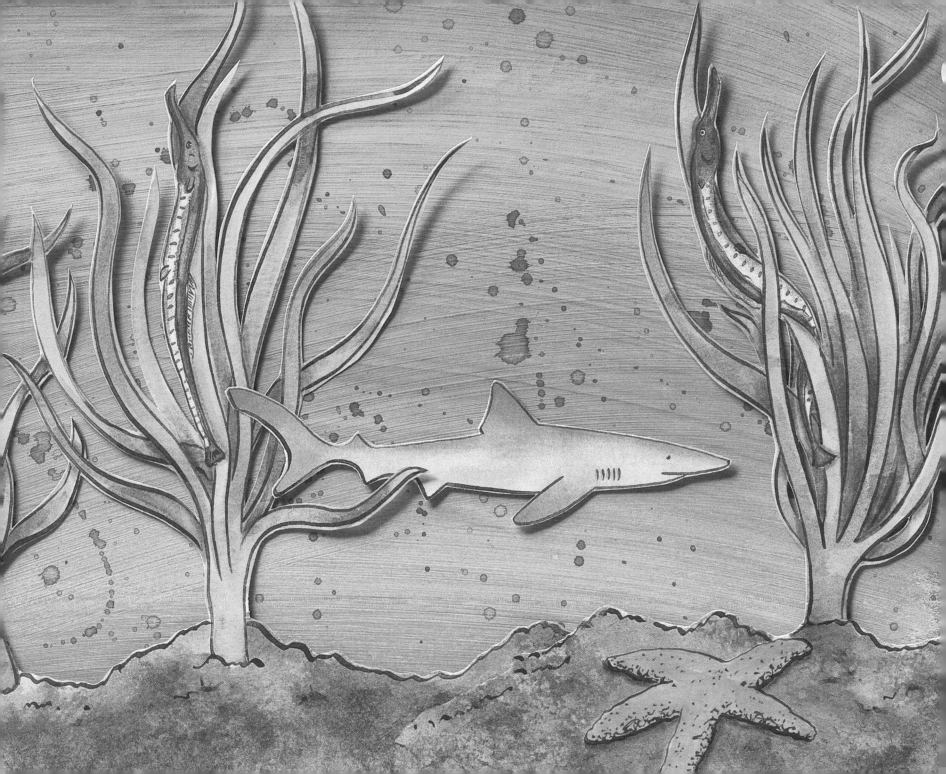

Swim fast, Little Shark!

This enormous sea is full of hungry sharks
that are much bigger than you.
They have plenty of sharp teeth
to gobble up smaller fish—even little sharks.

They can't chew,

so they bite off chunks of their

prey with their sharp teeth and gobble

the chunk in one swallow.

Little Shark is hungry, too.

Watch out, all you tiny fish! Swim fast!

Little Shark was born with plenty of sharp teeth.

Most animals have to keep their grown-up teeth

all of their lives.

But sharks can grow new teeth whenever they need to.

Sharks can feel the vibrations fish in danger make when they swim, even when those fish are far away.

Little Shark keeps swimming and swimming

in the deep darkness of the sea.

He usually stays below where the sunlight can reach.

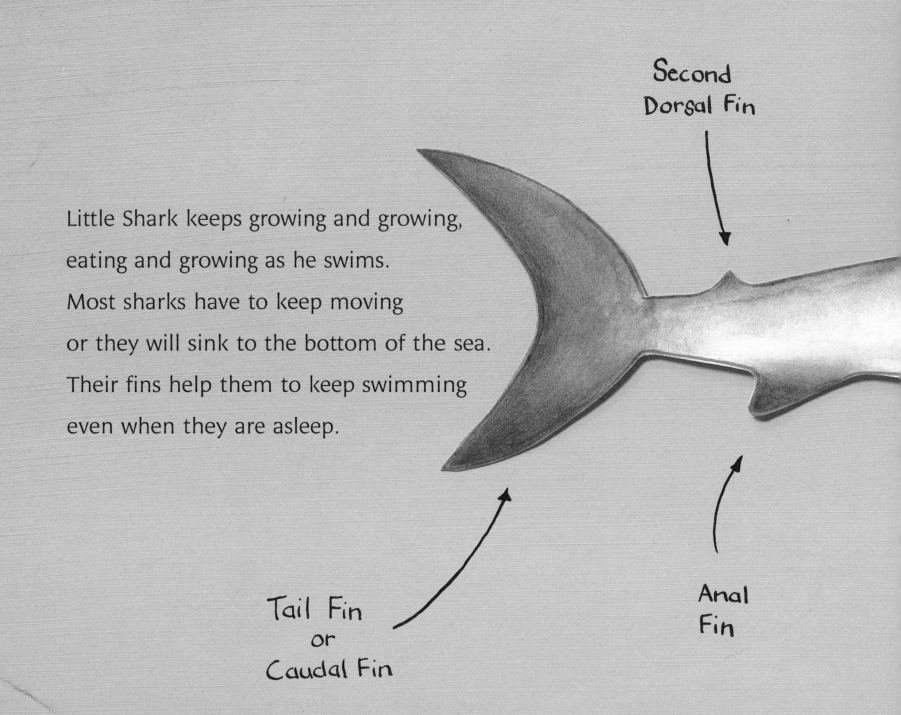

Second
Dorsal Fin

Little Shark keeps growing and growing,

eating and growing as he swims.

Most sharks have to keep moving

or they will sink to the bottom of the sea.

Their fins help them to keep swimming

even when they are asleep.

Tail Fin
or
Caudal Fin

Anal
Fin

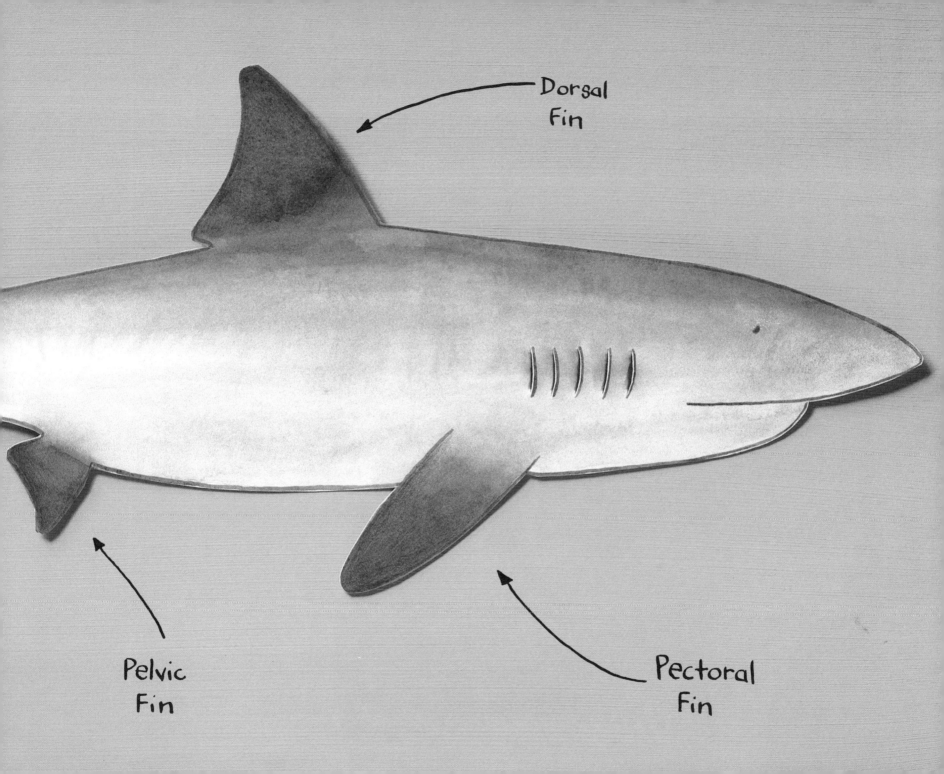

Dorsal
Fin

Pelvic
Fin

Pectoral
Fin

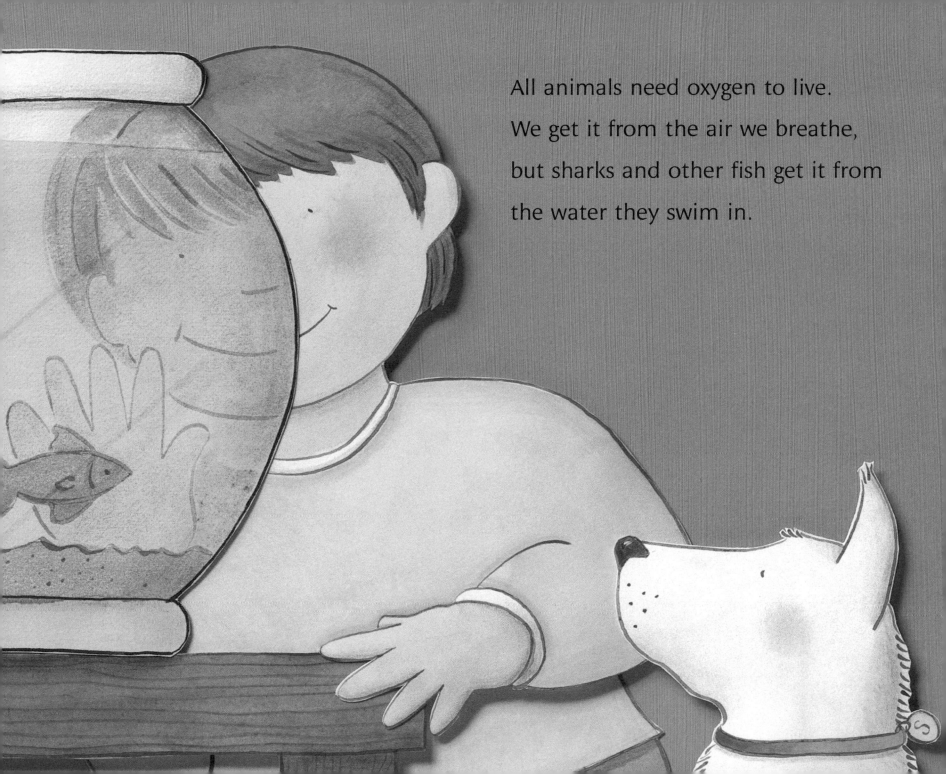

All animals need oxygen to live.
We get it from the air we breathe,
but sharks and other fish get it from
the water they swim in.

Most sharks have to keep swimming so water full of fresh oxygen can pass through their gills.

That's how they breathe.

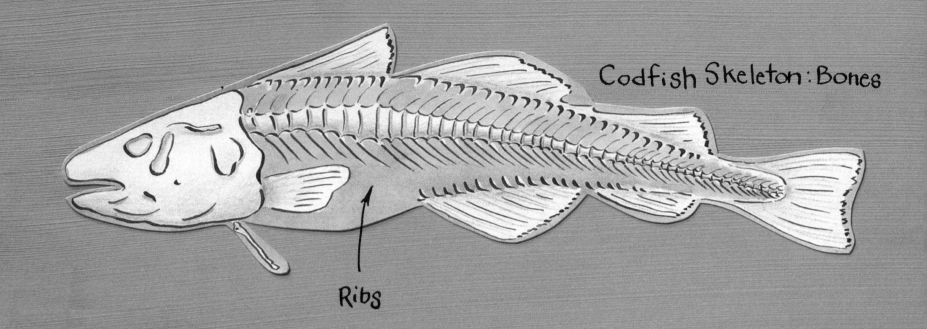

Codfish Skeleton: Bones

Ribs

Shark Skeleton: Cartilage

Gill Arches

Little Shark's skeleton isn't like the skeleton of other fish.

Other fish have hard bones.

A shark's skeleton is made of rubbery cartilage,

like the tip of your nose, not bones.

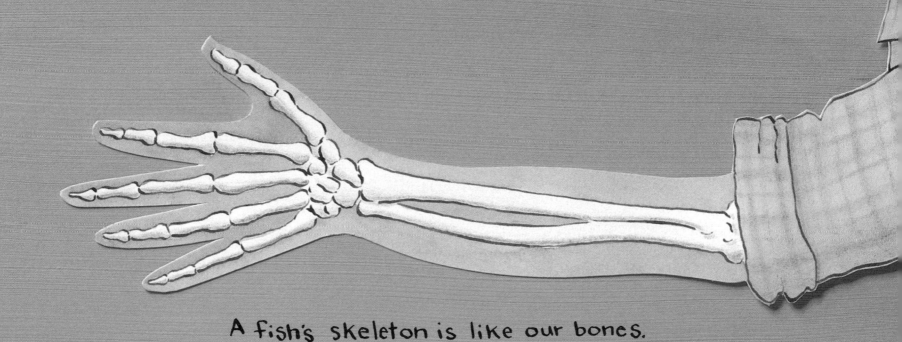

A fish's skeleton is like our bones.

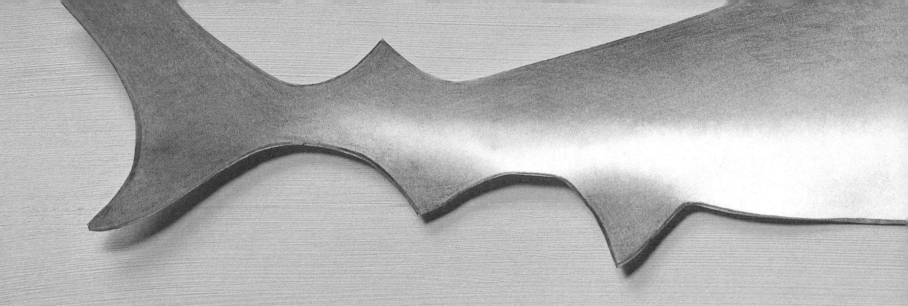

Little Shark doesn't have smooth and slippery scales

like other fish.

Sharkskin is covered

with thousands of tiny, curved sharp tips, like a shark's tooth.

Years ago, people used this rough sharkskin instead of sandpaper

to rub wood smooth.

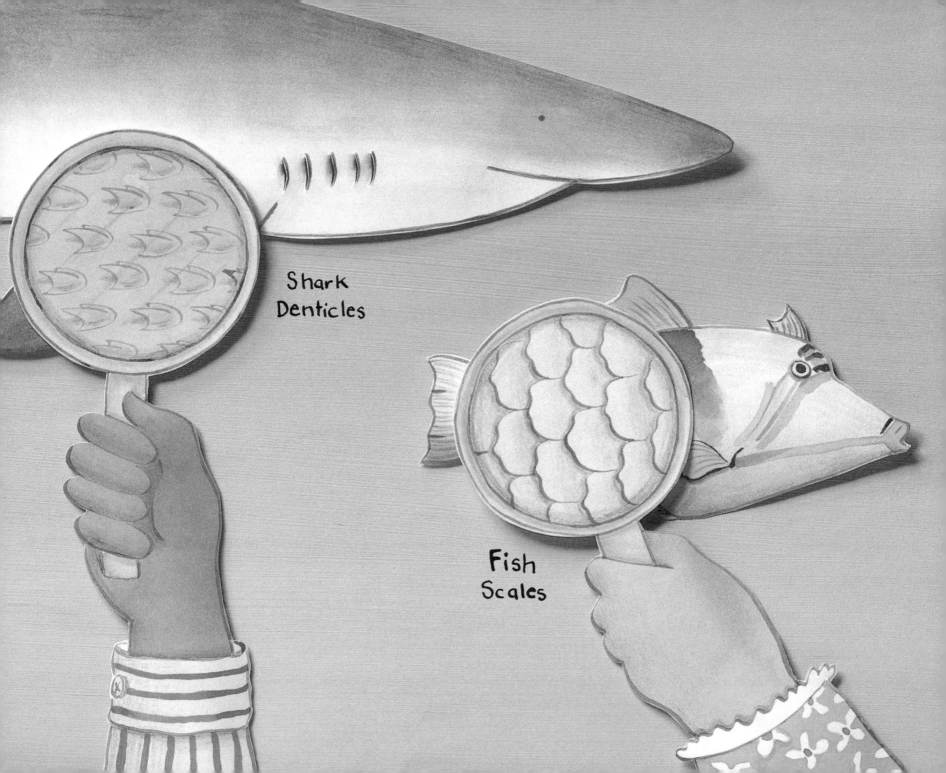

Shark
Denticles

Fish
Scales

Little Shark keeps swimming and eating,

eating and growing.

What kind of shark

do you think Little Shark will grow up to be?

A leopard shark?

A blue shark?

A hammerhead shark?

A great white shark?

A spiny dogfish shark?

Little Shark has grown into a **big blue shark!**

See—no big shark has caught him.

No fishermen has caught him either.

Little Shark will reach twelve to thirteen feet long,

as he keeps growing until he is old.

He will keep growing as he swims

all around the world.

Author's Note

Sharks are some of the most ancient animals living today. Four hundred thousand years ago, there were sharks similar to those that live today in the sea.

There are many different kinds of sharks, but I chose to make Little Shark in this story grow up to be a blue shark. They are beautiful, with their long, sleek bodies, blue on the back, fading to white underneath (although the intense blue color they are while alive quickly fades to blue-gray after they are caught).

Blue sharks are believed to be the fastest-swimming fish in the sea and are found world-wide. No one knows exactly how fast they swim, but scientists think their speed is between thirty-five and sixty miles an hour.

A female blue shark is able to give birth to pups by the time she is about five years old. She can have anywhere from twenty to over a hundred pups, but she usually gives birth to more as she gets older and bigger. Blue sharks live to be about twenty years old. Like many fish, they keep growing all their lives and can grow up to thirteen feet in length.

Blue sharks are predators, which means they eat other animals. Their favorite food is squid. Although they have hurt fewer people than many other animals, all the same, we should always be on the lookout for shark fins when we go to the beach and avoid swimming at night or in murky water. But human beings are the most dangerous enemies sharks have. Fisherman catch them on lines for sport, and they are often caught accidentally in the wide nets set out to catch schools of smaller fish.

If you're curious about these remarkably interesting animals, you can visit an aquarium, a safe place for people and sharks to observe one another.

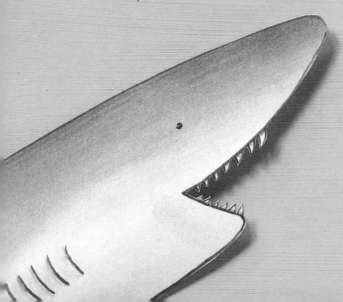